ORESTON and ITS PEOPLE REMEMBERED

Arthur L. Clamp

This early shipping scene shows the ferry boat, *Dart*, coming in to Oreston with the two-masted ketch, *Amy*, and the three-masted schooner, *Carmenta*, moored at Gutter in the background.

This version of the book is virtually as originally published.
There are now additional pages at the back providing information about the author.

The republishing project is being managed by Arthur's grandson, Steven Gibson. We aim to find all the research that he was involved in publishing, preserving it for the next generation as part of 'The Clamp Collection'.

THIS illustrated booklet of Oreston and many of its people is not intended to be taken as a history of this interesting village. Its main purpose is to make a permanent record of many of the main places, events and people which have taken place or lived here during the past eighty years. It should serve as a useful reminder of these now bygone scenes and inform the younger generations of Oreston what their place of living looked like during these years.

There have probably been more changes in the village during the past few decades than during the previous hundreds of years, changes brought about by the car, improvements in roads and bridges, and the very large amount of council and private housing estates that now cover almost all of the Plymstock parish area. Changes have also affected the pattern of local work, the older boats are no longer on the "mud", employment is less centred on the village, more people seek work in Plymouth and away from the area and so on. Social patterns have changed through radio and television, individual pursuits and local events and festivities are not so frequently undertaken. As one elderly person put it, "You can hardly recognise the place now, especially the higher ground behind Oreston which was once all fields and the village was quite separate from Pomphlett and Dean Cross." Many of the illustrations in this book will highlight these changes but through their inclusion with accompanying text their mark on the village and the faces of many of its former residents will less likely be forgotten.

The maps printed in this booklet will give readers a good idea of the extent of the village before the developments changed its size and character and the main reason why it is sited here, one of the settlements that grew up to serve commerce and trade associated with the sea. It must be remembered that when trying to picture the plan of the early village the contemporary developments and buildings now standing on the Cattedown side of the Laira were not there, the bridge linking this side to Plymouth had not yet been built and Oreston itself was quite a separate community even to Turnchapel, its waterfront neighbour. It will be seen from the earliest map that a well trodden crossing point from the then very rural areas of Plymstock and Wembury had been in use here since at least the 1200s which eventually led to the growth of the small community.

The old town of Plymouth had played a dominant role over hundreds of years in naval matters, journeys of exploration and discovery and trade across the sea to the New World and many other parts of the seven seas. Oreston played its part in these activities as well. Small and not so small craft have been constructed and maintained from these banks of the Laira, countless men have gone out from here to carry goods and bring back to their home port fish and goods needed to meet the requirements of a growing nation. The coastal shipping trade, the shipping of stone, lime, timber, etc. both to and from here, was almost the only means of employment for generations of Orestonians. Many, until very recent years, were known as "Captain . . . .".

This was one side of the life of the village; the other was the land-based activities. The village had its own farms, dairy produce was always available on request, the large number of quarries and the construction of the Breakwater, the timber yard now over 100 years old and the growth of small shops all made their contribution to the character of Oreston. In the wake of these came the chapels, schools, halls, the established church, the various inns, and the many small trades which served the everyday needs of the people.

This illustrated booklet can only show a very small percentage of some of these now bygone activities. Many were so common that it was probably thought that they were not worth photographing as they would always be here. But this has turned out to be otherwise. Many of the local events and people here lived long before the camera came into use so these parts in the story of Oreston have left no trace at all. However, because many people have hung on to their photographs, maintained an active mind in local affairs, a willingness to answer questions and offer advice about the early village, this booklet has been made possible.

I am indebted first to Mr. and Mrs. W. Gould who showed a greater willingness to help me furnish these illustrations with information than I could have ever hoped. Advice and other illustrations came from Mrs. E. Martin, Mr. Eric Andrews, Mr. Dick Oxland, Mr. and Mrs. H. Elford, Mrs. E. James, Miss K. B. Stephens and J. Tope, Mr. and Mrs. A. Cook, Mrs. D. Passmore and others who in one way or another contributed to the preparation of this title. Assistance was also forthcoming from the staff of the Plymouth Library and from a few correspondents away from this area.

I have endeavoured to check the information shown and to give as accurate a picture as possible of events of yesteryear. Any deviation from this aim is my own shortcoming and not the fault of others. This book is dedicated to the numerous people of all ages who have, through their work and manner of living, contributed to the life and character of Oreston over the last eighty years.

Jack Harper is seen here painting the mast of his fishing boat *Doris* at Oreston quay. The scene is 1925 and in the background are men seated at the "Oreston Parliament" to the right of the ferry boat.

Low tide at the old quayside when the dummy landing stage stood high out of the water. Note the cleared area beyond the *King's Arms* where Green Railings and other buildings used to stand.

Turnquay with the dummy landing stage in the background and Captain Ellis's whaler moored at high water in the foreground. The single stack of the old "dirt destructor" can be seen to the left of the mast on the site of the present power station.

This close up view shows one of the old ferry boats, *Rapid*, landing passengers at the dummy at high tide. Note the ironwork and gas lamp at the head of the landing stage leading to the original quayside and the then much smaller *King's Arms*.

The lower water landing stage or pontoon, built by the Elfords for taking on and landing passengers to and from their boats. This ran out from the wall at Gutter and was used at low tides when the dummy stage could not be reached by the ferries.

Low tide in the harbour with the ketch, Amy, moored alongside the now covered Gutter wall. On the left is the dummy landing stage and the end of Turnquay can be seen just to the rear of the ketch.

This very early photograph of the harbour and dummy landing stage reminded one local person of the days when barrels of beer were brought to Oreston by "Daddy Launder" on high tide by boat from Plymouth. They were simply thrown overboard where they remained until the tide went out. The licensee of the *King's Arms* then had to haul them up the steps on planks with rope and across the quay to the nearby cellars.

Postcards of local scenes are just one source of pictures as demonstrated by this view of the old quay wall. The post office and other buildings are clearly seen on the right and one ferry boat landing passengers is to the left.

These two old limestone buildings, which were part of the old waterfront, have had a very chequered use. For many years they have been used as small engineering shops. They were formerly used for boat building by Mr. Pile then for storing threshing machines when not in use by Mr. Clarence Elford. The machines were hired out to local farmers during harvest and were well known in the area.

This well-built limestone residence was known as *Green Railings* and stood facing the old quayside. It was demolished in 1958 with other buildings as part of the re-development of Oreston's waterfront by Plympton Rural Council.

A last look is taken at another of Oreston's once familiar old buildings before it fell to the force of a bulldozer in 1958. This large three-storied building stood behind the island and old custom house, one ground floor room of which was Mrs. Carder's general shop (behind the white panel).

This action photograph shows part of the old island house crashing down in late 1958. The building was a prominent landmark at Turnquay which had been used both for commercial and private purposes for many years. Generations of local people would have been very familiar with it overlooking the enclosed harbour.

This photograph includes both staff and scholars of the Oreston Wesleyan Sunday School probably taken on the same occasion as the staff photograph (see page 8) as part of the celebrations of 100 years service to the people of the village. No doubt many of the young scholars in this group will be recognised and some may well still be living in Oreston.

This group photograph was taken on the occasion of the Oreston Wesleyan Sunday School centenary in 1915. The officers and teachers were: *Superintendents*: T. S. Cooms, W. H. Coleman. *Secretaries*: W. Harper, P. T. Ellis. *Treasurer*: George C. Pillidge. *Staff*: J. Pope, C. Pillidge, W. Tope, Miss D. Kingwell, Miss D. Ellis, Miss G. Holberton, R. Brown, W. Jackson, R. Tolley, Miss A. Oliver, Miss Mary Ellis, Miss A. Davis, T. Lavers, J. Carter, Mrs. G. Tope, Miss F. Cooms, Miss E. West, Miss M. Holten, R. Moses, E. W. Brown, Miss Marian Ellis, Mrs. S.

Two scenes from the once very busy years when Oreston had many men and boats in local service. *PHE* stands for Peter Henry Eva. The boat belonged to F. J. Moore, quarry owner, and was used for coastal trade. The three men on the ferry are, from left to right, W. Parry, engineer, Captain Dick Oxland and the mate, W. Tucker.

SOME ORESTON FAMILIES

Many long standing Oreston families have come together through marriages over the years the names of which regularly occur in records and conversations. Here is one such occasion. The marriage is between Mr. R. White and Miss E. Dare seen with Mr. and Mrs. R. White and two daughters, Mr. B. White, Mr. and Mrs. J. Dare, senior, Mr. J. Dare, Miss E. Rickard, Mrs. C. Carder and Miss N. Carder with others in the early part of this century.

All set for an enjoyable carnival in the village in the late 1940s. The procession of vehicles and floats are seen here making their way up Plymstock Road.

Very high tides with flooding were not uncommon years ago as seen in this photograph. The two boy canoeists, D. Norsworthy and M. Smaldon, can be seen enjoying themselves close to the old quay wall.

Once a familiar item in the pockets of most local people — a return ticket issued by the O. and T. Steamboat Co.

"Up pump" were the words used by one senior citizen to locate these dwellings when shown this photograph. They were demolished to make way for the present buildings in Plymstock Road. One was once used for a time by Mrs. S. Edwards as a newspaper shop.

Can any of the children be recognised in this photograph of the inter-war years taken outside of Mrs. Carder's general shop? It occupied one room in the old three-storied building from about 1906 to 1933 and was demolished as part of the new waterfront area of Oreston in the late 1950s.

Timber is being unloaded from the *Pia* at Oreston during low tide. This was one of the first boats to bring in wood for use as railway sleepers and bridge supports at Bayly Bartlett's timber yard.

All ready to receive customers. Mr. William Morgan, an ex-Marine, is seen here in 1929 outside his barber's shop now Watts flower shop. All the signs bring back memories of goods many of which have long gone together with the old price for a haircut!

This almost unique photograph shows two char-a-bancs outside Oreston primary school in 1920. There were two others as well which were all about to set off to Looe to support an Oreston Rovers football match. Among those recognised here, starting from the left, are Mr. and Mrs. J. Algate, Mr. and Mrs. H. Cowell, Mr. and Mrs. W. Pile, S. Phillips, P. Ellis, E. Davis, A. Jackson, Master J. Algate, Master E. Passmore, F. Carder, W. Box, Mr. and Mrs. T. Harper. In or close to the coach on the right are Mrs. M. Booth and baby, W. Booth, A. Martin, F. Brooks, Mr. and Mrs. Ned Ashford, Mrs. A. Gould and Mrs. A. Martin. No doubt many others will be identified in this large group and bring back memories of those now far off days.

Keen supporters of Oreston Rovers are about to leave the village on one of their many trips during the 1920s. Some recognised here are Mary Edwards, Muriel Lavers, Mr. and Mrs. Wills, Arthur Martin, Mr. and Mrs. Hall, Mr. and Mrs. J. Algate, Joe Algate, Mrs. Billy and Clare Norsworthy, Sammy Phillips, Len Sargent, Gran and Grandad Brown, Clara Sargent, Joe Jackson and Mrs. J. Jackson, Mrs. N. Williams and Mrs. Sargent.

Prince Rock, an appropriately named local char-a-banc, is about to set out for an Oreston Wesley Guild's trip to Exmouth in July, 1927. Those seen are Miss A. Oliver, Miss G. Tope, Miss A. Tope, Miss V. Tope, Mrs. Young Husband, Miss Oliver, Mrs. Blackmore, Mrs. Kingwell, senior, Mrs. Curber, Mr. Row, Miss Johns and Mr. and Mrs. Rapson.

Another Rovers' supporters outing is represented here by Mrs. M. Brooks, Mr. and Mrs. S. Kingwell, Mr. and Mrs. W. De Viell, Mrs. W. Carder, Mr. and Mrs. W. Booth, Mr. and Mrs. R. White, Mrs. A. Edwards, Mr. W. Carder, Mr. and Mrs. H. Tall, Mr. J. Sprague, Mr. and Mrs. B. Mountjoy, Mr. J. Edwards and son, Mr. and Mrs. J. Nicholls and their two sons.

The upper photograph was taken outside of the Barrage Balloon hut during the 1949-50 season of the Oreston and District Rovers Football Club. Among those here are D. Strange, S. Dolton, E. Howard, P. Body, L. Lake, H. Spencer, D. Jackson, D. Warren, D. Carter, G. Osborne, A. Williams, B. Bolt, J. Weatherdon, R. Farnell, H. Williams, W. Gould, B. Norsworthy, C. Burres, G. Jackson, S. Weatherdon and others. The team below played during the 1951-52 season comprising of G. Jackson, W. Gould, D. Roberts, A. Pullinger, R. Sherrel, D. Squires, White, C. Burns and seated Spiller, E. Putt, Watts, F. Putt, Roberts and one other.

The upper photograph shows the Oreston Rovers in 1947-48 in which has been identified Messrs. Harrison, Bolt, R. Ryder, R. Oxland, Clark, Inch, S. Dalton, C. Burns, Clarke, P. Body, W. Gould, A. Harris, S. Weatherdon, Ryder, G. Jackson, B. Norsworthy, Harrison, J. Weatherdon, E. Howard, R. Farrell and D. Jackson. The next season's members can be seen below as R. Demelweek, S. Dolton, F. Parsons, P. Body, D. Squires, J. Harrison, G. Osborne, K. Carter, J. Weatherdon, D. Strange and R. Farrell.

his is probably one of the rliest photographs of Oreston overs which was taken during e 1899-1900 season. Among ose recognised are J. Langman, . Davis, Mr. C. Burch, r. S. Tope, Mr. W. Pile and . Carder.

The 1908/9 team, from th back, left to right: A. Townsend A. Kingwell (hon. secretary) A. Ellis, W. Couch, J. Edwards Arch. Ellis (hon. treasurer) H. Hooper, F. Bustin, E. Davis chairman. S. Oxland, Trainer G. Jessop, A. Shapter, J. Nicho son, J. Squire, Captain, H. Ellis T. Powell.

)23-24 team were winners Devon Senior Cup. They m the back, left to right: raggs, trainer, W. Pile, an, I. Leathlean, captain, ancock, L. Mitchell, cholls, hon. treasurer, son, trainer, J. N. Roose, nt, A. Ellis, R. Ellis, gler, B. Mountjoy, hon. ry, W. H. Whear, errifield, H. Jenkins, , A. Greenwood.

The former R.A.F. Barrage balloon billets once stood where Orchard Crescent is and were later used as recreational rooms by Oreston Rovers. One balloon was raised here during the raids. Devastation in Thornville Villas after a heavy raid with some residents making the best of the situation. A homecoming hug and welcome for Sergeant F. Tucker in 1945 from a prisoner-of-war camp in Germany. His wife is carrying their son Brian and among those flanking him are Margaret Elford, June Tapper, William Hill, Roger and Brian Axworthy and Michael Turpitt.

WARTIME AT ORESTON

Although Oreston was just outside the city area during the war years it did not escape all the wartime raids. It suffered considerable damage and loss of life during two major raids and from occasional bombs and small fires. Ten people were killed and two fire fighters during the first raid on Oreston on 28th November, 1940. Four houses were demolished with loss of lives. The second major raid was, in fact, the last on Plymouth and took place on 30th April, 1944. A stick of four bombs covered the area killing eighteen people in the village and injuring a further thirteen. Three women wardens were among those killed. A direct hit was made on a shelter tearing up the main gas pipe along the road as well. The Cattewater and the large contingent of troops awaiting landing orders to enter France and the oil storage tanks at Turnchapel were good targets for enemy planes.

Oreston and District Bowling Club, 1934, showing, left to right, H. Wright, H. Williams, J. Davey, J. Hunt, D. Ruffin, D. Frost, W. Featherstone, W. and Mrs. Gould with H. Gould, Mrs. S. Kingwell, Mr. McKroskie, Mrs. C. Elford, Mrs. Thomas, Mrs. McKroskie, Mr. Thomas, J. Hocking and C. Elford.

The Over 60 Club annual dinner in the Church Hall in 1952. Mrs. L. Ellis, Mrs. J. West, . Carter, Mr. Lord, Mrs. and Mr. Roberts, Rev. R. Forward, Mr. Cavendish Lamb, W. Gould, G. Jackson, Mrs. G. Oxland and Mrs. S. Rogers.

Oreston and District Bowling Club, 1931, showing, left to right, W. Coleman, C. Elford, Lt. Com. Crocker, C. Palmer, C. Hockaday, D. Howie, S. Kingwell, W. De Viell, J. Brimacombe, Mr. Hamilton, D. Frost, W. Bullen, C. Shillabeer, Seated are Mr. Thomas, Mr. Hamlyn, H. Wright and W. Gould.

Mrs. M. Rapson is seen here standing in front of Bayly's Farm sometime in the 1920s, now a private dwelling in Plymstock Road. Like all the local farms milk and cream could be bought here and was purchased from Mr. and Mrs. Charles Holten years ago.

This photograph of a metal plate was taken from a cyder press still in use near Tavistock. The small foundry of R. Doddridge worked from the old buildings still standing by the quay although the business had long ceased before the turn of this century.

The old pump in Plymstock Road was one of the focal points in the village especially at Sunday dinner times when people queued for a jug of its sparkling fresh water. This was a regular practice even after piped water came to Oreston. It was the main source of water for the inhabitants and it was usually the duty of the children to collect the day's supply of water before and after school. The granite trough no doubt provided plenty of fun when full as children tried to duck one another. A Mr. Robert Hawkins, who lived opposite, was the self-appointed and recognised guardian of the pump and it was only through his efforts that it was not immediately dismantled when piped water was introduced by the Plympton Rural District Council.

This 1950 photograph shows members of the Oreston Methodist Girls' Club under the leadership of Mrs. Connie Cooke whose daughter, Sandra, is crowned as Queen. Also to be seen are Maureen Carder, Linda Cooke, Karen Dwyer, Jennifer and Tina Hawkins, Diane Richard, Heather Sprowell, Elizabeth, Tracey and Helen Tope and Wendy Weeks.

Mr. and Mrs. James Dare are seen here in their later years when both had retired from an active life in the area. Mrs. A. Dare was the local midwife and, no doubt, many present adults owe much to her care and attention when they first saw the light of day. She was very well known and lived for some years in Green Railings.

Bazaar time for the Friendly Circle, some of whose members were Mrs. C. Cooke, Mrs. I. Groves, Mrs. P. King, Mrs. D. Lobb, Mrs. S. Rickard and Mrs. D. Roberts. It still meets each Wednesday at 2 p.m. at the Methodist Church, and Mrs. B. Williams was its President at this meeting in 1950.

TRADE DIRECTORIES

The information shown on this page was taken from various directories whose date is printed alongside each one. Many of the names have long gone but they do give a good indication of the changing pattern of commercial life of the village.

ORESTON.

Clergy.

Scovell Rev. John Frederick, B.A. (curate of Plymstock)

Trades and Professions.

Avery Mrs. Elizabeth, lodgings, Burt's cottage
Pillar James, grocer and coal merchant
Bayly and Fox, timber merchants and steam saw mills ; and at Coxside
Ballhatchet Thomas, foreman to Messrs. Bayly and Fox
Barker Thomas, master mariner
Blackler George, marine store dealer
Brooks Richard, baker
Coombs William, carpenter, grocer, and draper
Dean Richard Arthur, baker and grocer
Elford Henry E., butcher and farmer
Holloway Brothers, patent fuel merchants —Samuel Taylor, agent
Hurrell Mrs. Ann, "Old Inn"
Jeffery John, farmer, Quick farm
Jordan Thomas, coaldealer and lessee of ferry
Kingswell Mrs. Mary Ann, "Foresters' Arms"
Pile Mrs. Caroline, "King's Arms"
Skinner Richard, beer retailer
Spencer John, marine store dealer
UNDERHILL GEORGE DAVID, ship and boatbuilder, Oreston. (See advertisement)
Wells Mrs. Caroline, shopkeeper
Wills Edwin, limestone and ballast merchant, Oreston Quarries and Quay
Wright William, master mariner

Post Office—William Damerel, sub-postmaster. Letters from Plymouth arrive at 7.30 a.m. ; closes at 5.25 p.m. on week days ; Sundays at 12.40 p.m. Plymouth is the nearest money order office

1870

ORESTON.

Bayly R. & R. timber merchants & railway creosoting, Kyanizing wrks
Body Dart, butcher
Carder Edith (Mrs.), shopkeeper
Colman William H. carpenter
Coouns Miriam (Mrs.), farmer, Quicks farm
Cooms Thomas S. builder, Post office
Elford Sidney A. builder
Ellis Harriet (Mrs.), shopkeeper
Ellis Thomas, baker & grocer
Harper William, draper
Holton Charles, farmer & butcher
Lucas William, boat builder
Masonic Lodge (Sir Walter Raleigh, No. 2,958) (William Henry Start, Stadfold, sec)
Oreston & Turnchapel Steam Boat Co. Ltd. (Henry Emanuel Elford, managing director)
Pile Emma L. (Mrs.), King's Arms P.H
Reid Thomas, butcher
Ridge Priscilla (Mrs), rate collector
Tope Samuel, assistant overseer

1910

Oreston.

Lewarn Samuel John

COMMERCIAL.

Bayly R. & R. timber merchants & railway creosoting, Kyanizing works
Bowden Robert, Foresters' Arms P.H. & dairyman
Carter Samuel, shoe maker
Cooms John, grocer, Post office
Cooms Miriam (Mrs.), dairy
Davis John Henry & Co. ship brokers
Edwards John, baker & grocer
Elford Henry Emanuel, butchr. & farmr
Ellis Philip, coal merchant
Holten Ann (Mrs.), baker
Lucas William, boat builder
Oreston Steam Boat Co. (Henry Emanuel Elford, managing director)
Passmore Elizabeth (Miss), shopkeeper
PileSl. Edwd. King's ArmsP.H.&boat bldr
Rudd Elizabeth (Mrs.), baker
Sparrow & Co. quarry owners
Williams James, butcher
Willis Edwin, quarry owner
WorkingMen'sHall(ThomasReid, mng.
Williams John, apartments

Oreston.

Bayly Robert & R. timber merchants
Bowden Robert, Foresters' Arms P.H
Carter Samuel, shoe maker
Cooms John, grocer & general dealer ; burning oils at lowest prices, wholesale & retail, Post office
Cooms Miriam (Mrs.), dairy
Dean Catherine (Mrs.), baker
Edwards John, baker & grocer
Elford Henry E. butcher & farmer
Ellis Philip, coal merchant
Oreston Steam Boat Co. (E. R. Jones, manager)
Passmore Elizabeth (Mrs.), shopkeeper
PileSl.Edwd.King'sArmsP.H.&boat bldr
Rudd Elizabeth (Mrs.), baker
Sparrow Lewis, quarry owner
Williams James, butcher
Willis Edwin, quarry owner
WorkingMen'sHall(Wm.Brown, mangr)
Williams John, lodging house

1889

ORESTON is a hamlet of this parish, on the banks of the Catwater, one mile west from Plymstock, containing the extensive stone and marble quarries of Messrs. J. and E. Goad, and the steam saw mills and timber yard of Messrs. Bayly and Fox. The stone of which the breakwater is formed was quarried here, and a cavity was found in the rock 60 feet deep, containing bones of the rhinoceros, wolf, deer, &c.

Town Sub-Post. M. O. & T. Office, Oreston.—Thomas S. Cooms, sub-postmaster. Letters through Plymouth delivered at 7.30 & 11.30 a m & 3 30 p.m. ; sundays at 7.30 a m ; dispatched at 8.45 a.m. & 12.30 & 6.5 p.m. ; sundays, 8.45 a.m

1893

Post & M. O. O., S. B. & Insurance & Annuity Office, Oreston —John Cooms, sub-postmaster. Letters through Plymouth, delivered at 7.30 a.m. & 12.30 & 4.15 p.m. ; sundays at 7 30 a.m.; dispatched at 8.45 a.m. & 12.45 & 5.50 p.m. ; sundays, 12 noon. Castledown is the nearest telegraph office

ORESTON.

Hodge, H. C., Esq. | Neville, C. T., Esq., Government inspector, Oreston Quarries

TRADERS, &c.

Brooks, Elizabeth, baker and grocer
Dean, Amy, baker
Dinnes, George, farmer
Dodderidge, John, blacksmith
Elford, Thomas, farmer and butcher
Kerswell, Richard, farmer
Oxland, Benjamin, lessee of ferry
Passmore, John, lime and coal merchant
Pearse, John Quick, farmer, Quick farm
Perry, Samuel, merchant
Pile, John, victualler, King's Arms
Pillage, Robert, stonemason
Pillar, James, baker and grocer
Taylor and Wright, merchants
Vivian, Richard, marine stores
West, William, postmaster

1862

POST-OFFICE, Oreston.—Mr. W. West, sub-master. Arrival, 8 a.m. ; despatch 5.40 p.m. Nearest money-order office, Plymouth.

Town Sub-Post, M. O. & T. Office, Oreston.—Miss Florence May Cooms, sub-postmistress. Letters through Plymouth

ORESTON.

Elford William Henry, Raleigh

COMMERCIAL

Carder Edith (Mrs.), shopkeeper
Coleman Wm. Charles, undertaker
Coleman William H. shopkeeper
Cooms Florence May (Miss), shopkeeper, & post office
Cooms Thomas S. builder
Cooper Irving, motor car proprietor
Elford Clarence C. thrashing machine owner
Ellis & Lawson, bakers
Ellis Edith (Mrs.), shopkeeper
Frost Ellen J. (Mrs.), shopkeeper
Holton Charles, farmer
Lawson Wm. baker, see Ellis & Lawson
Lucas William, boat builder
Masonic Lodge (Sir Walter Raleigh, No. 2,958) (Phillip Bateman, Plymstock, sec)
Oreston & Turnchapel Steam Boat Co. Ltd. (William Henry Elford, managing director)
Pile Emma L. (Miss), King's Arms P.H
Plymouth & Oreston Timber Co. Ltd. timber merchants, & railway creosoting, Kyanizing works
Rogers Fredk. Percy James, tailor
Simmons George Henry, builder
Stribling Lewis Thomas, butcher
Tope Samuel, assistant overseer

1923

Christmas dinner for the Old Folks' Club during the 1950s. Mr. Ayre, Mr. Welcose, Mrs. White, Mrs. Dare, Mrs. Ellis, Mrs. Coles, Mr. White, Mr. Carder, Mrs. Phillips, Mrs. Norris, Mrs. Oxland, Mr. Townsend and Mr. Lord have been identified in this photograph.

Winnie Ellis outside her hardware and drapery shop in the early 1930s. It was originally a fish and chip shop and then came under the present owner 46 years ago.

This very fine engraving dates from the late 1820s and is entitled *Oreston and the Cat-Water near Plymouth*. It captures what must have been a common everyday sight of various craft at or moored near the different quays.

Members of the Oreston Ladies Bowling Club can be seen above against the background of the school. The ground is now built over where this scene was taken during the late 1930s. Mrs. Shillabeer, Mrs. S. Kingwell, Mrs. C. Elford and Mrs. De Viell have been recognised in the group. The men's Oreston and District Bowling Club group was taken in 1950 and comprise of *rear row*, R. Seeds, C. J. Burns, F. Mumford, W. C. Bassett, F. R. Bullivant, R. Bryant, W. R. Gould, *centre row*, F. Shillabeer, O. Curphey, W. C. Simpson, D. Moncur, C. W. Rowe, R. C. Sergeant, G. Jackson, W. Barretto, R. T. Tucker, H. V. Hasler, F. Fletcher, F. J. Bunker, *front row*, A. R. Martin, *vice-captain*, H. J. Williams, *captain*, A. J. Davey, *vice-chairman*, F. Mardon, *vice-president*, S. O. Kingwell, *president*, C. W. Rowse, *chairman*, R. Symons, *hon. treasurer*, G. H. Frost, *hon. secretary*, J. Brown.

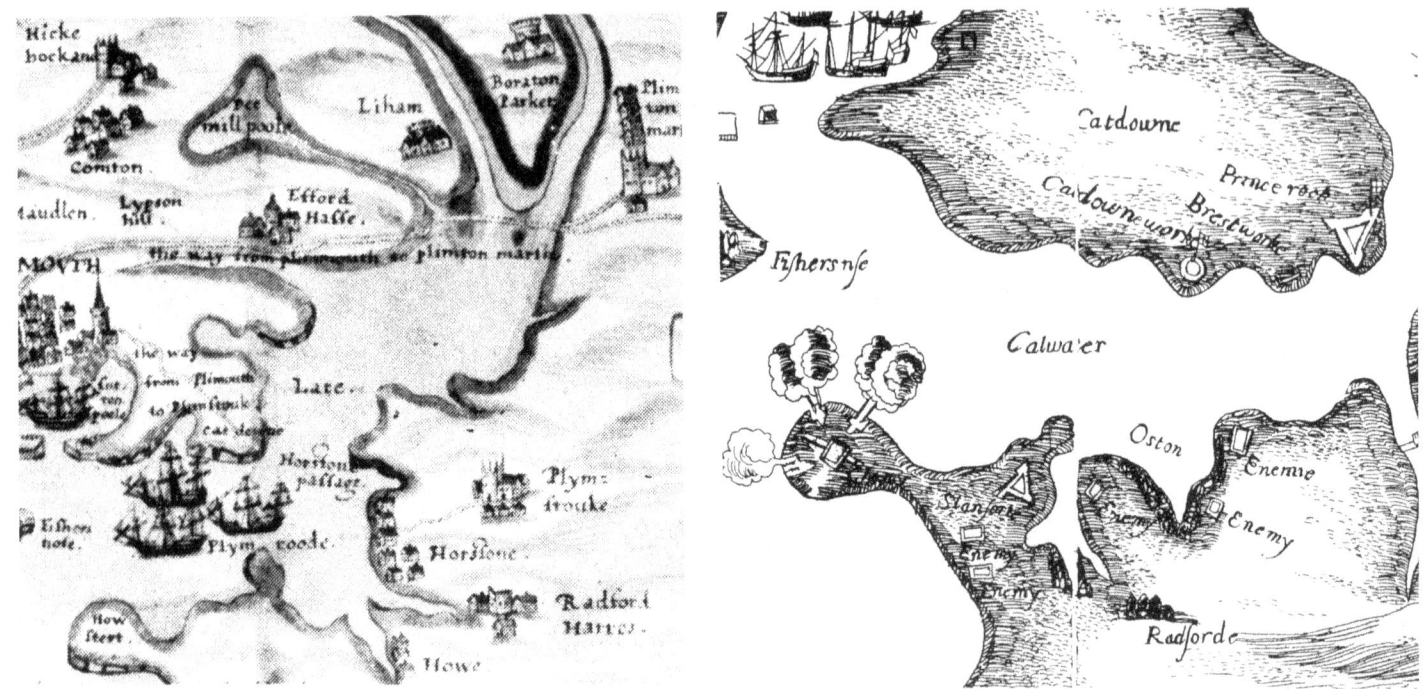

These early maps of the Cattewater and Oreston area show quite clearly the absence of buildings in the locality prior to the last fifty years. The earliest map was produced in the 1590s and shows *Horstone Passage*, the crossing point from Plymstock to Cattedown, the birthplace of Oreston village and the reason for it being sited here. *Ostun* is shown in the Civil War map of the 1640s in which the enemy or Royalist positions are indicated with an active battery at Mount Batten. The more detailed map is dated 1915 which gives a good picture of the village as it was during the past hundred years or more before the housing developments and the changes of more recent years.

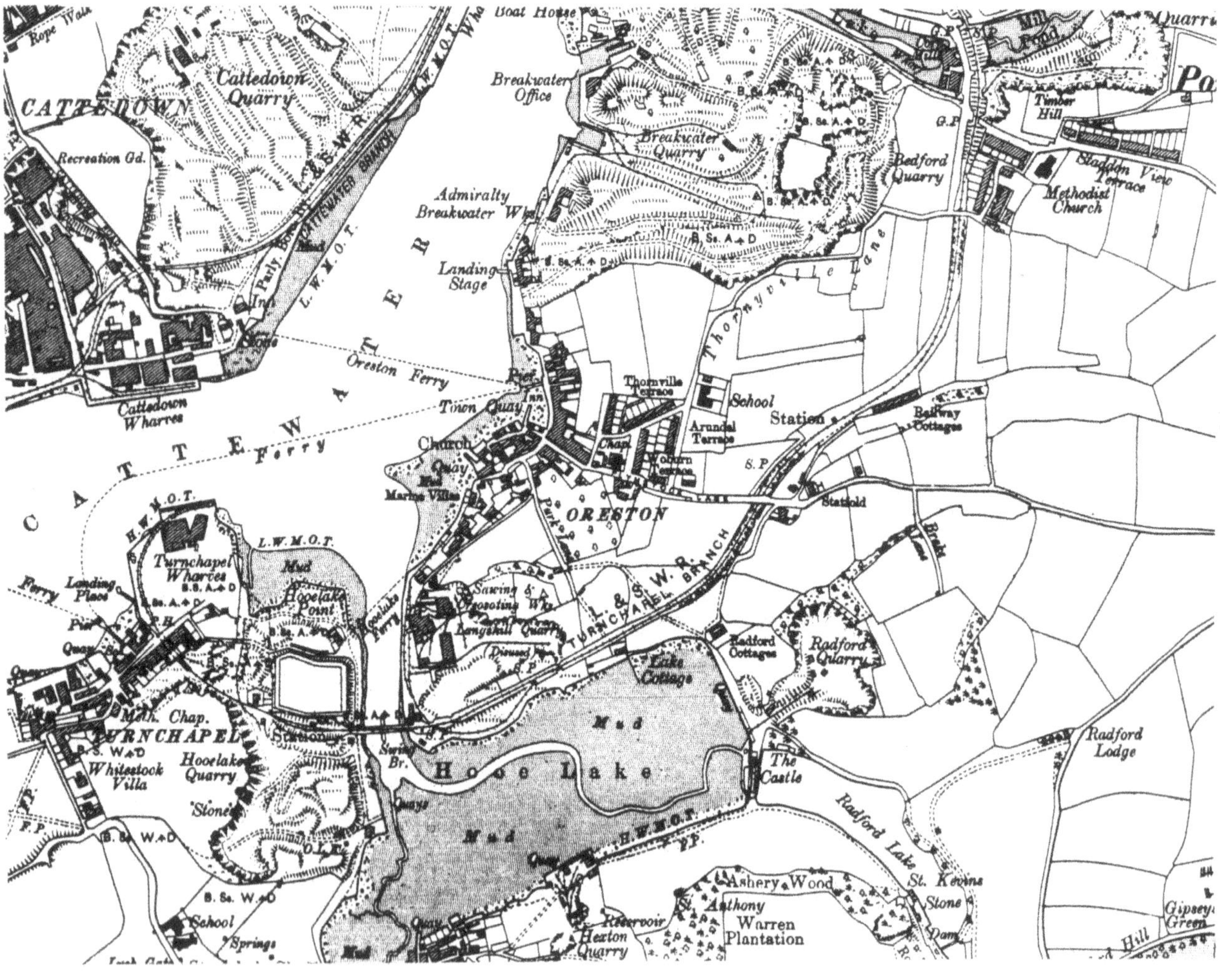

Arthur L. Clamp – the man behind the books

Arthur Leslie Clamp was a man of boundless energy with a passion for helping others, particularly through his love of history. A printer by trade, he started his career in a printing company before moving his family from Exeter to Plymouth to teach at the Plymouth College of Art and Design, where he eventually became the Head of the Printing Department.

Arthur with his five children.

A Devoted Family Man

Despite his love of teaching, Arthur prioritised his family, always making it home by 5:30pm for tea. He and his wife, Rosemary, raised five children: Susan, Angela, Elizabeth, David, and Steven. Arthur would often combine his love of family and history by taking his children on Sunday walks, encouraging them to appreciate historical monuments by taking photos or making crayon rubbings of gravestones for his books. The family home at 203 Elburton Road was a hub of activity, with a large garden, featuring a two-storey fort and a makeshift swimming pool.

A Lifelong Learner and Adventurer

Arthur's thirst for knowledge extended beyond history to a deep curiosity about the world. He was passionate about exploring different cultures, traditions, and cuisines, often taking advantage of his long summer holidays as a teacher to travel to places like India, Russia, South America, the middle east and the USA, sometimes bringing one of his children along. This adventurous spirit even influenced his home life, as seen by the short-lived family tradition of steam-cooking vegetables after a trip to Iceland.

History is a prominent feature of family days out

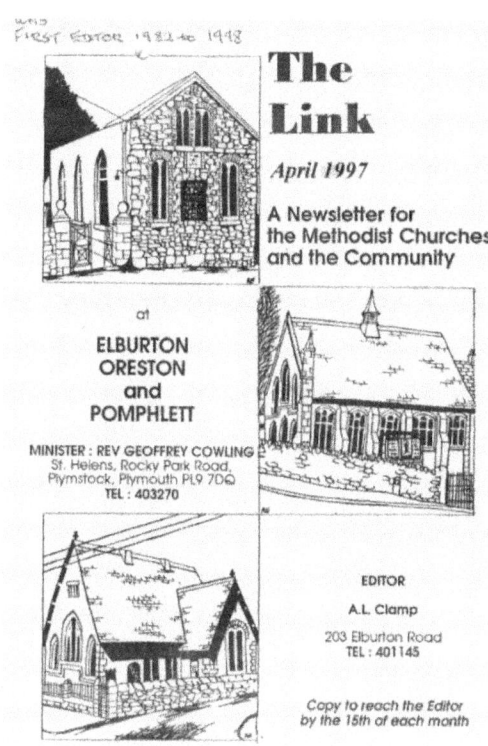

Community and Philanthropic Spirit

His commitment to serving others was evident in his long-standing involvement with the Elburton Methodist Church. He was the Sunday School Superintendent for over 15 years and served as the editor of the wider church's monthly newsletter, "The Link," for a similar duration. After Rosemary's very sad passing, Arthur later remarried and, following a chance encounter with a professor from India, established a connection with a missionary school in Chennai. Together with his new wife, Christine, he co-founded a "Sponsor a Child's Education" program that continues to this day.

*Pictured left – The cover of 'The Link' complete
with hand drawn sketches of each church by Angela
Below right – Arthur Clamp promoting his latest book
Below left – Arthur at home with his first wife, Rosemary
Below centre – Arthur on holiday with his second wife,
Christine*

A Legacy of Learning and Positivity

Arthur's greatest passion was history, which he brought to life through tireless research, documentation, and the many books he authored. He was driven by a need to "never be stuck in a rut," constantly seeking new experiences, meeting new people, and expanding his knowledge. With a positive attitude and a great sense of humour, he was always ready to help others, leaving a lasting impact on his family and community. His children, Susan, Angela, Elizabeth, David, and Steven, remember him with love and gratitude.

David Clamp, 2025

A Legacy of Local History

Below is the story of how Arthur L Clamp began writing books, in his own words, drafted shortly before he passed away in 2001. I have only made minor alterations to this text, correcting grammatical errors that he did not survive to correct himself. When I first discovered this text, I was shocked to see my name mentioned. It seems that, unbeknownst to me, I shared my first PC with him. I suspect he used it during the day when I was at school, although I do have one memory of sitting with him and showing him how it worked. It has been a pleasure to pick up where he left off and see his books republished and redistributed, and to know that I was part of the story, even back then. It was also fascinating to discover that his pricing structure matches the way I have tried to price the books, with a third going to local sellers and the rest covering printing costs with a little left over for my expenses.

I am his eldest grandson, and it is a privilege to curate his legacy, which we are calling 'The Clamp Collection'. The very last line of the text originally reads "The following pages list all the titles." Sadly, that page is missing and we have no record of all the books he published and knowing that some of those were researched by other authors makes the process of finding them even harder. I look forward to one day completing the collection and seeing them all available again. And maybe, one day, I'll even start writing my own to add to the series. For now, here is his story in his own words.

Steven Gibson, 2025

Writing and Publishing Booklets on Local Topics and Areas

I started this interest in either 1968 or 1969 when living in Woodford. I had by these dates established the Department of Printing and I think I must have been looking for something different to do. The first titles were of A5 size proofed from type set at Clarke, Doble and Brendon, Ltd., Plymouth printers, and then made up into pages and printed at Sawtell and Neilson, Ltd., Totnes.

Then began a slow process of getting them out to shops, etc. which proved to be more time consuming and difficult than actually researching, writing and getting the books into print. However, I persisted and opened a business account with Barclays Bank on the Broadway. I was advised to give it a title so I called it "Westway Publications". There came along another problem, one of storage of paper and finished books which was solved when the family moved to Elburton in 1970.

I changed the printer to Penwell, Ltd., Callington, Cornwall, as he was then just setting up himself and his prices seemed very reasonable. I did not get any of the printers to make up the complete books. I hand folded the flat printed sheets, stitched the books on a small manual table stitcher and trimmed them in a small hand turned guillotine which I bought from someone in Penzance for £40. It was brought up in a van.

The trouble and time going to and fro to Callington was too much so I transferred the printing to PDS Printers, Prince Rock, Plymouth, and I have been with them ever since. Now they are at Plympton which is easy to reach and they fold the flat sheets which was turning out to be a long chore which only saved a small part of the printing costs.

All my first titles were written by myself. I took the photographs and developed them in the loft of the house, the type was set by now on a computer situated in the house at Elburton from which I had collected photographic lengths of text to cut up and law down as pages.

At some point I decided that I would do my own film processing of lith film so I bought a large second hand process camera from Kingsbridge and learnt through trial and error to make line negatives of the text and halftone negatives of the illustrations which proved more difficult than I anticipated. The main problem was trying to keep the developer in the large dish at the correct temperature as any change would affect the developing time. I replaced this old camera with a brand new one bought from Croydon, Surrey, costing £900. This has turned out to be a great asset cutting out an expensive part of the printer's costs and one crucial aspect of the work which I could control.

By the middle 1970s there were many outlets I had contacted in Plymouth, up to Dartmoor, Exeter, around to Torbay, Totnes, Dartmouth and the South Hams. The market for local books was much greater than I had first thought and through getting to know many local people undertaking research themselves had the chance to help and make up books for other people who had in most instances, got together a collection of photographs with some text in a rather muddled way. Through my experience in print I was able to shape up their work and get it into print and in every case I had to pay the printer and let the person have the royalties. In the majority of titles produced in this manner this was another way of producing titles and it did give some profit to my work. However, I must say that in a few cases I lost out by either the other person getting the numbers wrong, not returning any monies from stock I delivered or they thought that more of their books should have been sold.

The print run was usually 1,000 copies and from time to time I have had reprints of 250 copies. It took about ten years to clear the first print run so I always had large stocks in the garage, workshop, etc. The numbers sold during the early years was about 7,000 copies a year increasing to around 9,000 copies and for the whole of the enterprise about 500,000 have been sold. The booklets have become part of the local scene and many people collect them, shops regularly order copies and I go around certain areas month by month restocking or replacing titles as necessary.

During the past year or so I have started setting the text on a Packard Bell PC, something which I should have done some years back. I share it with Steven Gibson, my grandson. There appears to be no end to the market for local books, but I could not earn a regular income because of the long time it takes to sell stock.

However, now exceeding 100 titles made up mainly of A4 twenty-four page booklets, some folded guides, with selling prices set with a third going to the shop which is the trade custom, the original idea has been quite successful and could go on for ever.

Apart from monetary benefits, however spasmodically these might be, I have learnt a lot myself, met many interesting people and have become part of the local scene with requests to give talks and to advise people about getting into print.

Arthur L Clamp, 2001

This newspaper article, published by the Evening Herald on 17th August 2001, forms a good record of his life. Just as he encourages us to learn more about local history, we encourage you to learn a little about him. For that reason, we have included these pages at the back of all the most recently republished books, in honour of his memory and recognition of his contribution to the community.

www.ingramcontent.com/pod-product-compliance
Lightning Source LLC
Chambersburg PA
CBHW061407070526
44584CB00031B/4184